An Introduction to Coping with Post-Traumatic Stress

Ann Wetmore

ROBINSON
London

Constable & Robinson Ltd
3 The Lanchesters
162 Fulham Palace Road
London W6 9ER
www.constablerobinson.com

First published in the UK by Robinson,
an imprint of Constable & Robinson Ltd, 2010

Important note
This booklet is not intended as a substitute for medical advice or treatment.
Any person with a condition requiring medical attention should consult
a qualified medical practitioner or suitable therapist.

ISBN: 978-1-84901-410-6

Printed and bound in the UK by Thomson Litho

1 3 5 7 9 10 8 6 4 2

Contents

About This Booklet

Traumatic events are so extremely stressful that most people find themselves completely overwhelmed for a short while, and often for some time afterwards. In the space of a few seconds, the impact of a catastrophic experience can turn lives upside-down, and leave people disoriented, anxious and in a state of disbelief about what has just happened. Situations such as car crashes, robberies, job loss after years of loyal employment or sudden death of a loved one can be very difficult to cope with, and may leave us numb or angry and closed off for days or weeks until life settles down again.

If you've gone through a terrible experience and found that the intense reactions that you had from it refuse to go away or that pieces of the memory continue to interfere with your life, this booklet may be helpful to you. The material in this booklet is meant to serve as a starting point, to help you to understand your reactions and to put in place some new coping strategies. It's likely to be most useful for people whose post-traumatic reactions came from a single event where they experienced horror, loss or injury. Those who have unfortunately been caught up in long-term traumatic situations, such as domestic violence, physical and sexual abuse, hostage-takings, or combat situations may find this material a useful beginning, but are likely to need additional professional help to deal with their complex post-trauma feelings and reactions.

If you (or someone you know) have been suffering with issues of post-traumatic stress, Part 1 of this booklet will help you gain a clearer understanding of your reactions and why they are not going away. Part 2 contains practical strategies for you to work through by reading, writing and reflecting on your thoughts and behaviours. This material was designed for you to work through on your own, but if, at any point, it feels like too much for you to continue with alone, please talk to your doctor about additional resources, which may include help from a qualified therapist, or medication.

While it's natural to wish for an instant answer or a 'magic' solution, many post-traumatic conditions are so complicated that healing becomes a lengthy and uneven process, with gains and set-backs to be expected. Go slowly, but keep working at it!

May all your efforts lead to healing after your trauma.

Ann Wetmore

A Cautious Reminder

This booklet is intended as a self-help guide and as a first step in managing post-traumatic stress symptoms. It's *not* a 'magic' answer in itself, nor is it a total representation of all treatment possibilities. It's also not a substitute for ongoing therapy with a trained professional. It may be very useful in getting you started on a recovery route, and helping you to understand better what has been contributing to your distress after trauma. It's hoped that the booklet will be a practical, readily available resource to have on hand while you're waiting for a referral to a treatment programme, or as a home-based workbook to supplement sessions with a practitioner in cognitive behavioural therapy. If the cognitive behavioural approach, on which this booklet is based, does not feel like the right 'match' for you, or if you feel your symptoms are in any way worsening while you're using this material, please speak openly about this to your doctor and explore other options through the healthcare system.

Part 1: ABOUT POST-TRAUMATIC STRESS

1 What Is Post-Traumatic Stress?

Most of us expect to have some stressful events happen in our lives, preferably one at a time. When we're called upon to perform under difficult circumstances, meet challenges and deal with disappointments and crises, we may feel alarmed at first, but usually we can muster up our coping resources, tough it out, and get through it. The difference with a traumatic event is that the experience is so extraordinarily stressful that it goes beyond anything we ever expected to happen, or anything we could have thought of as 'normal' and been prepared to handle.

Because traumatic events are both terrible and terrifying, if you have had such an experience – like being a passenger in an awful car crash, receiving a violent assault or witnessing a severe workplace injury – you probably felt overwhelmed and horrified. Your body may have gone into shock, combined with surges of adrenaline, and you may have acted as if you were stuck on 'auto-pilot'. For days or even weeks after the incident, you may have had difficulty concentrating, been unable to sleep for any length of time, and perhaps you found yourself replaying the incident over and over in your mind, or having nightmares about it. You may have continued to feel numb, like you're 'going through the motions' but not really 'there', and you may have tried *not* to think about it, or found yourself obsessively thinking about it all the time. All of these descriptions are very typical post-traumatic stress responses. Usually, after some time has passed, the reactions gradually subside – the incident is not forgotten but ceases to interfere, for the most part, with everyday life.

'Why me? Why can't I get over it?'

Two people can go through the same experience – for example, a nasty accident – and their perceptions of how traumatic the incident was may be quite different. That's where the *meaning* of the event comes in: one person may say, 'I thought I might be hurt, but I didn't think this was the end', whereas another might say, 'Time stopped and I thought, "This is it . . . life is over!"'

Cynthia's story

Cynthia was involved in a cycling accident, where a car hit her and she found herself hurtling through the air, over the front of the car and hitting the road with her body sideways. She suffered a broken arm, multiple scrapes and bruises and a severely swollen face. Although both the ambulance attendants and, later, the hospital workers, assured her that her injuries would heal, and that there would be no permanent damage, she was convinced that she would never be the same again. Over and over she had memory flashes of seeing the gravel and dirt of the road coming up to hit her face, and she was afraid to even look at her mangled bicycle. For months she had nightmares about being attacked and harmed.

Her friend, Jane, who had also had a cycling accident some weeks before, kept trying to boost her confidence, saying, 'You'll get over this, and as soon as you're able to ride again, you'll be fine! I just got back on my bike as soon as possible and now I don't even think about it.' Cynthia didn't find this helpful, as she wanted her own physical injuries to heal before working on her emotional ones, and to re-build her sense of a 'personal safety zone', whether walking or cycling. The meaning of the experience had been very different for both girls, and much more traumatic for Cynthia.

'Is there any pattern to my symptoms?'

PTSD is the only condition that is diagnosed as the result of something having happened to you, an event that you experienced that was so catastrophic that 'life changed in a heartbeat', as some survivors have said. There must have been a real or perceived threat to your survival or to your personal safety and the way that you understand natural justice – in that moment of horror, you felt your very existence to be at risk. People will usually recount such experiences with statements such as:

> I really thought I was going to die' . . . 'I didn't think we would make it through' . . .'I thought I was a goner'. . . 'I could not believe it was happening – it was so horrible and I couldn't stop it!' . . . 'I thought I would split apart!'

'I have some of those symptoms but not all of them – does this mean that I don't really have PTSD?'

There are three main types of PTSD symptoms, which are interconnected, like the sides of a triangle:

◆ intrusion   ◆ arousal

◆ avoidance/numbing

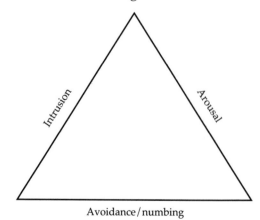

Avoidance/numbing

Like all triangles, this arrangement is very stable – it can tip over on to another side without changing the overall balance. So at one point, one set of symptoms may be bothersome and the next, another may take over your attention . . . but the post-traumatic stress goes on and on.

Symptoms of post-traumatic stress disorder

Intrusion

◆ Flashbacks – you feel like the trauma is literally happening all over again, often with vivid sensory experiences of sound, smell, sight, etc.

◆ Intrusive memories – you get vivid memories of pieces of the traumatic event; you can't stop thinking about certain aspects of the experience; horror images keep popping into your mind as if your brain is stuck there.

◆ Upsetting dreams/nightmares – your dreams may be like re-living the experience in sleep and may connect to the arousal symptoms below, as you wake sweating and terrified; your nightmares may be worse than what actually happened, as they may symbolize your worst fears or represent the deepest terror connected to how you felt during the event.

◆ Memory 'triggers' – small occurrences in everyday life, such as a sound, smell, a look on someone's face or a news broadcast, may set off a chain of memory 'bits' and the distress reactions associated with them.

◆ Feeling 'triggers' – sometimes referred to as 'feeling flashbacks', where being in an anxious/aroused state that resembles feelings you experienced during the traumatic event (for example, being squeezed and jostled by the crowd while waiting to get on a train) will trigger reactions such as profound fear, twitching or a sense of utter helplessness that's an over-the-top response to the current situation.

Arousal

◆ You feel keyed-up or 'hyper' all the time.

◆ You're uncharacteristically irritable; you have angry outbursts or outraged confrontations with others, which is not like your normal self.

◆ You're constantly scanning for danger and you startle badly when surprised by something trivial.

◆ You can't fall asleep – you're afraid to sleep, and have difficulty staying asleep or going back to sleep when wakened.

◆ You have problems concentrating or focusing on tasks, which you didn't have before the trauma.

Avoidance/numbing

◆ You make serious efforts to avoid any thoughts, feelings, persons or activities that could remind you of the trauma, even those very remotely linked to the event.

◆ You change your behaviour so that memories of the trauma won't be triggered.

◆ You pull away from others; you feel set apart: *'I don't have the words to tell you what happened to me.'*

◆ Your emotions feel numb and unavailable; you can't react properly to your loved ones and feel isolated: *'I'm not the person I was before.'*

◆ You don't look forward to the future any more.

You don't need all of these symptoms to be diagnosed as having PTSD. Sometimes one set of symptoms will be much more active, for example, feeling on 'red alert' all day, even without flashbacks or avoidance; or having many flashbacks and 'mini-memory-flashes' even when you're consciously not avoiding any part of your normal activities.

For some, not getting a full diagnosis of PTSD will affect whether they receive legal compensation or qualify for disability or injury claims. Obviously diagnosis requires a full assessment from several qualified practitioners, and you shouldn't make assumptions on your own from the list on the previous page.

Regardless of whether you have all the signs, or whether some symptoms and behaviours that you didn't have before the trauma are now having a terrible impact on your life, it's important that, rather than waiting and hoping for these feelings to just go away, you look for effective ways to manage what's going on and begin to claim your life back. This booklet is unlikely to be the final solution, but it may serve as a powerful first step in helping you determine your needs and your future, and it may help you to communicate better with your doctor and others about your condition.

'How do I know if I have post-traumatic stress disorder? I think I'm going crazy!'

According to the widely accepted medical definition of post-traumatic stress disorder (PTSD), your symptoms must have continued for at least a month for you to be considered to have PTSD. Sometimes people have delayed traumatic reactions – they feel fine at first, for a fairly long time, and then a second stressful event might trigger a whole series of reactions that had been suppressed. Those whose symptoms never go away or whose post-traumatic stress reactions emerge long after the event and suddenly interfere with daily living often are people who are really good at coping and who have never encountered any situation they could not overcome with hard work and determination. It's profoundly upsetting to them to find themselves 'losing control' and being at the mercy of intrusive memories, nightmares, angry eruptions or feeling like they are strangely removed from everyday events and loved ones. They will usually try to keep their worst fears to themselves, wonder if they are 'going crazy' and fear they will 'never get over it'.

If these questions and concerns have arisen for you or for someone close to you, the material in this booklet will provide a starting point to help you to recognize and understand some of the causes behind those post-traumatic stress reactions. Realizing that they're happening because you experienced an extreme circumstance (and not because you're going crazy) is the first learning step in beginning to manage the reactions.

Helen's story

'I had been involved for a long time with a man who was very abusive to me, physically and emotionally, and, after I separated from him, it took several years of counselling at the Women's Centre in my community for me to really feel I was in control of my life and that I had come to terms with understanding and getting past the post-traumatic stress reactions that had been with me for so long. Then, recently, out of the blue, while I was running on the treadmill at the gym, a man bumped into me from behind by accident, and I fell on the still-running treadmill, and was horribly scraped and bleeding, and I thought my elbow was broken. The two staff on duty at the gym that evening were both young and had only been working there a few weeks – they didn't contact the manager and I had to drive myself, in a dazed condition, to the hospital, where I waited for several hours in the emergency unit before I was seen. Although it turned out that my elbow was only badly bruised and my scraped skin did heal, in the weeks that followed, many of my PTSD symptoms returned: I was jumpy, nothing felt safe, I was very emotional and hyper-reactive to anything that startled me, and I had a lot of trouble sleeping. The worst trigger was that I had felt physically hurt and completely helpless, and no one took me seriously at the time.'

Part 2: COPING WITH POST-TRAUMATIC STRESS REACTIONS

2 Cognitive Behaviour Therapy: What Is It?

What can I do about all these PTS reactions? I don't think I'll ever get over it. I just want to feel "normal" again!

Many effective treatments have as a basis cognitive behaviour therapy or CBT, as it's known. CBT focuses on identifying and changing your thought patterns, because it's believed that your thoughts, and how you interpret situations, influence your emotional reactions and that your behaviour follows from this.

It works like this: if your perception of a situation is distorted and produces exaggerated thoughts (*'Everyone is looking at me and laughing while I'm waiting in this queue'*), the feelings that arise almost simultaneously are uncomfortable and negative, and may result in you leaving the situation early and avoiding similar situations in the future. If you're able to recognize this and *change* what you're thinking, different feelings and behaviours are likely to follow.

How CBT works

CBT is based on an idea that thoughts, perceptions, feelings and reactions occur in a circle, like this:

Thoughts influence *perceptions* influence *feelings* influence *reactions* influence *thoughts*.

I find it hard to accept that my thoughts influence how I feel and that if I can change my thoughts, I might react to things differently.

Although it's true that the explanation of how CBT works *sounds* almost too simple – change your thoughts and you can change how you react emotionally – in reality, this is not about thinking positive thoughts and everything will be okay! The CBT process requires attention, focus, some serious commitment on your part and some recording work with pencil and paper, to raise your awareness of those rapid, almost-automatic thoughts that trigger debilitating emotions. Let's face it, if it was so easy and obvious, you would already have done it! The important thing to remember is that it can work for you if you give it a serious try.

Let's examine a type of 'near miss' from a CBT perspective. In this example, let's say you were *nearly* hit by a vehicle while crossing at a busy intersection when you were doing everything properly, that is, obeying traffic signals,

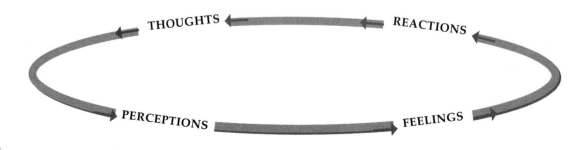

THOUGHTS ← ← REACTIONS ←

← PERCEPTIONS → FEELINGS →

12

crossing at a marked pedestrian walk, looking both ways before venturing out, etc. Despite all your good efforts, a van comes screeching around the corner at high speed, and barely misses you! Let's say it was such a close call that your jacket was brushed and torn by the van as it roared by, and you had to stagger to get your bearings and stay upright.

How would you feel immediately afterwards? Most likely, you would somewhat shaken, agitated and probably looking to see if someone else had witnessed this outrageous event.

What would you be thinking? Perhaps thoughts like: 'It came out of nowhere!' . . . 'I could have been killed!' . . . 'That driver is crazy!' . . . 'Why doesn't somebody do something?'

Does it make a difference if anyone else was there . . . if anyone comes over to help you? What are your thoughts and feelings then? Sometimes, if others validate our experience and reactions, it helps us make sense of the situation and not stay stuck in the heightened emotions.

What do you do afterwards? Do you tell anyone at home? At work? Do you repeat the story to friends? Do you immediately want to go for a drink to steady your nerves?

How do you interpret the event? As a lucky close call, or as a sign that no matter how careful you are, bad things will happen to you ('I'm jinxed!')? Your interpretation, how you think about what happened, positively or negatively, will likely influence how you feel about it later.

The table below shows two contrasting ways in which you may be thinking about the event.

You probably realized, in reading each of the two versions, that the statements would promote very different emotional reactions: the person with the positive interpretation would likely feel an affirmed sense of confidence, and may carry on thinking, 'I can trust myself to cope in bad situations.' On the other hand, the person with the negative interpretation might feel very defeated, and would be prone to superstitious thoughts like, 'It's futile to try, I'm jinxed!'.

Although these are extreme examples of 'all-or-nothing thinking', as it's sometimes called, it's clear from this illustration that the CBT method of writing down the thoughts and reflecting on them is key to changing negative thought patterns and the feelings arising from them. Part 2 of this booklet will help you to put this method into action.

Positive	Negative
'Someone' is looking after me!	Bad things always happen to me!
I have really good reflexes – I leant out the way just in time!	It's only a matter of time before something gets me!
I survived a very scary experience!	Nothing is safe!
Well done me!	'Someone' is out to punish me!

3 Starting Your Self-Treatment Cognitive-Behavioural Programme

You'll need:

◆ a notebook to write in

◆ safe surroundings to work in

◆ safe time limits

Your notebook

This can be of any size or shape, made with lined or unlined paper, and sufficiently robust to last through a number of weeks of daily entries. You'll be doing a lot of *self-monitoring*; by that we mean keeping track of your thoughts, feelings and behaviour, recording them in your notebook, and re-reading what you've written in order to reflect on it, recognize patterns and to make small goals that you can target. Because this is a very personal recording activity, you'll need to safeguard the privacy of your notebook, and ensure that it does not fall into the hands of others at times when you have not given them permission to read it. Locate a secure place – that could be a locked drawer, a suitcase or a filing cabinet with a lock, or even an inexpensive toolbox from a building supply store that can be locked. Respect your own right to privacy, and make it easy for others to do so by not leaving your personal writing out in the open and available to curious eyes.

Safe surroundings

It's important that you have some privacy when you're working on these recovery tasks. It can be difficult to find many uninterrupted moments if you're living in the midst of a busy family, or if your living situation is crowded and chaotic. Do what you can to reduce stress in your living circumstances, and to find a spot where you can use your notebook unobserved, even if that means that you need to work in short bursts and reflect later on what you've written.

If you're finding things chaotic, it may be tempting to consider a drastic change such as moving, selling your home or leaving your job. However, unless there are dramatic reasons behind these considerations (such as dangerous surroundings, threat of bankruptcy or violence in the home), it's usually best to postpone major decisions if possible, while you concentrate on relieving some of your post-traumatic distress. If you're in doubt, consult a trusted professional (maybe start with your family doctor) and don't be hasty about your decisions, as the PTS symptoms tend to 'move' with you, if unresolved.

Safe time limits

Set yourself time limits for your self-monitoring notebook work, and stop immediately if you become unduly upset. Ten or twenty minutes at one go might be enough, or you may be able to work for as long as an hour sometimes. It will likely vary from day to day, but it's recommended that you don't exceed an hour at a sitting. This is a process that's intended to *do no harm* to yourself or to others, so you must take careful responsibility not to do too much at one time and to keep yourself safe while you're dealing with volatile feelings. It's best not to do your writing work really late at night, as you're likely to reduce your chances for a sound sleep when you're emotionally wound up.

Managing your breathing

Obviously, you've managed to breathe on your own all your life! Because this is such an automatic function, you likely pay little attention to it, and you may fail to notice how much your breathing rate changes during stressful circumstances.

Runners, athletes, those who practise yoga, speech makers, exam-takers, etc. will all confirm that they had to learn to pay attention to their breathing rate, and sometimes to change the style and depth of their breathing to perform more effectively. We're going to use this same principle to teach you to 'tune into' your breathing and practise using it as a calming, stress-reducing technique. Although it's not a solution in itself, managed breathing is a very valuable tool in your personal CBT programme and available to you at any time.

At times, especially as a young person, when you got over-anxious or over-excited, you might have been told, 'Just take a deep breath', or 'Take a few deep breaths'. That was probably easier said than done! When you're anxious, your chest muscles tend to tighten up and your breathing becomes shallow. Air reaches only the top part of your lungs! When you're trying to gulp in more air, it feels impossible, and can result in short, rapid breaths that raise your anxiety level, rather than lowering it. There's a more effective way to control your breathing and achieve the desired result, a slower, deeper breath – it's called the '4–5–6–push' method (see the box below).

The '4–5–6–push' breathing method

1 *Exhale first.* Purse your lips and blow out through your mouth, like you are blowing through a wide drinking straw. Push out as much air as possible

2 *Inhale* through your nose to the count of four: 1–2–3–4

3 *Hold* that breath to the count of five: 1–2–3–4–5

4 *Breathe out* through your mouth, exhaling fully, to the count of six, then 'push' that last bit of air out at the end: 1–2–3–4–5–6 **push**

5 *Breathe in* through your nose again, letting your body automatically take this breath in more deeply to the count of four: 1–2–3–4; **hold** to the count of 5; then **breathe out** to the count of 6

6 *Continue* until you've finished three complete breaths

With each complete breath, you'll notice that the air is reaching more deeply into your lungs, and feels like it's going further down into your belly. Your breathing rate by the end is probably slower, and your heart rate has likely stopped racing. Use the 4–5–6–push breathing method whenever you notice that you're getting tense or anxious, or struggling to manage your feelings in difficult situations. Just three complete breaths with this method are enough to help you clear your head and gain a bit more control over your reactions in the moment.

Self-assessment: How are you coping now?

Think over these questions thoroughly and write your answers in your notebook.

◆ How has your coping behaviour changed since your traumatic event?

◆ Do you sleep? How well? Do you have nightmares or vivid night-time recollections?

◆ Has your temper changed? Are you getting into arguments with others, or even anticipating an argument?

◆ Do you drink more than you did before? How much more?

◆ If you've been prescribed medications, are you taking these properly?

◆ Can you finish tasks?

◆ Do you find it unusually hard to be intimate and loving? Are you avoiding friends?

◆ Are you living in the past, and re-living the trauma? Are memories haunting you?

◆ Are there certain things about that traumatic experience that you're keeping to yourself, that you've never told anyone?

◆ Are you 'fibbing' to your doctor about how well you are, or leaving out important health details or symptoms that you're worried about?

◆ Are you fibbing to yourself? Are you living in fear?

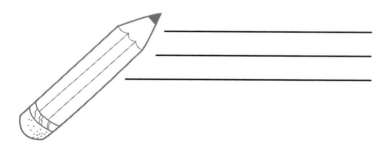

Recording phase

You do not need to answer all of the above questions in one sitting. There may be some that take more pondering, and you may need to come back to this 'coping self-assessment' at times and adjust your answers, or even record how you might have improved (or worsened) over time. Be honest! Because different areas are targeted, some may get better with attention, and some may go in the opposite direction. The goal here is to help you pinpoint your specific problem areas and assist you in developing improved ways to manage them.

Reflection phase

◆ Look over what you've written in your notebook. Pick out one or two areas that you would rate as the worst; that is, what's troubling you the most? Is it flashbacks, or memories that intrude while you're awake and trying to get on with things? Can't sleep or having nightmares?

◆ If you say, *'I just can't cope!'*, that statement is too vague – you need to be more specific. What is it that you can't cope with? When are you most overwhelmed? Are you hypersensitive to noise or over-reacting to every little thing that startles you? Are you angry all the time?

◆ Designate a reaction area to target and form a simple goal, for example: *'I will keep track on a calendar or in my notebook of how often I have flashbacks, and rate them from 1 to 10 about how severe and debilitating they are.'* Note the time of day that they occur, and identify any triggers that may have set them off. The table on the opposite page is a good example of how to do this.

Situation	How I reacted	How intense	How I felt afterwards
Fireworks outside at New Year's Party	Flashback to explosion/trauma	8 out of 10	Embarrassed – I dived under the dining table!

Coping with flashbacks and intrusive memories

Whether they occur during daytime or in the middle of a dream, flashbacks feel like you're re-living the trauma all over again. Sights, sounds, smells, the sense of things rubbing against your skin, all seem to be happening *now*, in the present time. Intrusive memories are like pieces of your traumatic experience that repeat and repeat and repeat. You're aware that they're remembered fragments but, because they're such disturbing memories, they *intrude upon*, or take over, your thinking when they occur. Both flashbacks and intrusive memories can last for different lengths of time (even a few seconds or a few minutes can be very disturbing) and the memories, especially, often differ in how intense and upsetting they are. It may feel like your mind is stuck on replay of certain scenes and that you're powerless in your struggle to get past these pieces of automatic recall.

Why do they happen? Flashbacks seem to come out of the blue and take over, so that you feel you're out of control, or even losing your mind. There are some theories that describe flashbacks as your brain continuing to try to make sense of a traumatic experience that was so overwhelming when it happened that there was no frame of reference for your mind to be able to file it away, or relate it to anything you knew or expected before. Thus, the raw experience keeps repeating over and over in your brain: images, smells, sounds and feelings from the traumatic incident that violated your assumptions about life and natural justice.

Although right now you may feel at the mercy of the memories popping into your mind, it's not hopeless! Beginning to pay attention, tracking any patterns, understanding how intrusions are set off and recognizing any triggers can help you to re-establish even a tiny bit of your sense of control.

Triggers

Here are two real-life accounts from individuals who had struggled to cope with flashbacks and intrusive memories. Following highly traumatic experiences, both Paul and Carla had been in treatment for PTSD for some months with a cognitive behavioural therapist and later described what had been most helpful in getting them to recognize triggers and move towards recovery.

Paul's story

'I had a lot of flashbacks and intrusive thoughts and terrible images (some worse than the actual trauma) that kept coming into my mind. Once I accepted that these were not necessarily true or accurate, but were actually symptoms of PTSD, my thoughts changed. Instead of thinking, "I'll never get over this", I started to think, "This is normal for me, right now." "There's nothing wrong with me . . . this is a symptom, and I have to pay attention to what triggered it." I no longer got into that cycle of worry and fretting about the flashbacks and images. When I started to think about them as symptoms, it became more about what I was doing to set them off, like when I aggravate my bad back and I have to figure out what triggered that back pain.'

Carla's story

'I came to regard my flashbacks and intrusive memories like "unfinished business" that my brain was trying to get me to understand. What was most helpful to me was to repeat to myself over and over, "This is a memory – it's not happening now!" I tried to ground myself in the present and pay more attention to sights and sounds around me that helped me focus on the here and now. I also deliberately reduced my exposure to potential "triggers" by not going to movies or watching TV programmes that I anticipated would have distressing scenes, even if they were only remotely related to the trauma I had gone through (such as watching violent situations with people being helpless). I kept my surroundings as calm as possible and watched very few news reports for quite a long time.'

4 Tackling Disturbed Sleep

Almost all the people who describe the after-effects of traumatic experiences report that their sleep was disrupted for some time after the incident. Many survivors are afraid to go to sleep, because they find themselves re-living their traumas through horrific, vivid dreams or through nightmares. If you're having sleep terrors like this, the content could be different from what actually happened to you, but the bad dreams may touch indirectly on your deepest fears (such as *'I dreamt I was about to be killed by a hooded assassin'*), and the terror you lived through. If your sleep has been disrupted for weeks or months, it has likely had devastating effects on your own functioning and your intimate relationships have likely suffered as well. If you're waking drenched in cold sweat, and your sleeping partner says you've been thrashing and calling out through the night, you're left feeling embarrassed and responsible for unconscious reactions that are impossible to control, and the bedroom may feel like an unsafe place for you both.

It's very tempting to turn to alcohol, hoping it will help you to suppress your feelings and recollections and also serve as a sleep aid! Unfortunately, over-drinking is not an effective form of sleep medication – it tends to add one problem on to another. You may fall asleep, but you're likely to wake in a few hours anxious and disoriented, and if you get back to sleep later, you'll still be having bad dreams. The after-effects of the alcohol contribute to depressed feelings and the temptation to drink more to block those out may be strong.

If you're trying to cope with disturbed sleep that's part of your post-traumatic stress reac-tions, it's vital that you scale back your drinking or give up altogether for a period of time. If that seems impossible, consider visiting one of the many organizations (such as Alcoholics Anonymous) that offer valuable support for reducing or stopping drinking. As the name indicates, Alcoholics Anonymous keep your identity anonymous and have helpful literature available, both in print and online.

Sleep medications may be an occasional or short-term solution but should only be prescribed and monitored by your doctor. Refuse recreational drugs and be cautious about the use of over-the-counter products that claim to regulate sleep. Often they are not very effective for people whose sleep problems originate with post-traumatic stress, and it's tempting to overuse them, rather than to ask your family doctor about underlying issues. Never take anyone else's prescription, whether for sleep disturbance or anything else.

Keeping a sleep diary

Your notebook can serve as a 'sleep calendar', or 'sleep diary' in which you record the patterns of your sleep, a week at a time. Draw seven blocks, one for each day of the week (or insert a pre-prepared calendar page), and use these to write:

◆ a number rating (0 to 10) for the quality of your sleep the night before (*'I would rate that a 3 out of 10'*)

◆ an estimate of how many hours sleep you did get, even if the sleep was broken (*'about three and a half hours altogether'*)

◆ how you felt when waking in the morning (*'exhausted'*, *'discouraged'*)

◆ any occurrence that you can identify, however small, that may have contributed to a terrible dream later or served as a trigger for a sleeping flashback.

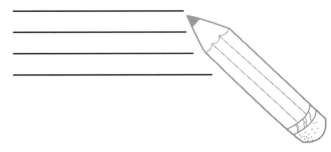

Here's an example of how your sleep diary might look:

DAY	Monday	Tuesday	Wednesday	Thursday	Friday	Saturday	Sunday
RATING:	3/10	4/10	4/10	2/10	4.5/10	2/10	4.5/10
HOURS OF SLEEP:	3.5	4	4.5	3	5	2.5	4.5
I FELT:	upset	exhausted	terrified	hopeless	numb	agitated	confused

THINGS THAT HAPPENED:

Monday, I ran into a former co-worker and tried to avoid conversation.

Wednesday, I was walking by a shop and I saw a jersey in the window like the one I was wearing on the day the trauma happened. I felt really upset.

Friday, loud noises at the pub got me really shaking.

Changing your 'sleep attitude'

Yes, you're being asked to take on the role of becoming your own 'sleep detective'! As you've probably already realized, when you're sleep-deprived it has a devastating effect on your mood state and your ability to concentrate effectively. It's very easy to slip into negative thinking, especially in that all-or-nothing pattern mentioned earlier.

> I'll never get over this!' ... 'It's hopeless' ... 'I can't go on like this' ... 'I'll be messed-up like this forever!' ... 'I'm no good to anyone'

Saying or thinking things like this to yourself can promote destructive impulses and risky behaviour, such as reckless driving, tempting fate by walking alone at night in unsafe areas, careless crossing of the street in heavy traffic or depriving yourself of food as a way to punish yourself. Take yourself out of harm's way by committing to suspend those 'always-or-never' habits of thinking and begin to 'observe' on paper what's really going on with your sleep.

Becoming a bit more objective and keeping notes about your sleep patterns provides clues to help you form an improved coping plan. Rather than merely saying that you'll continue to carry on and tough it out, the same way you've been doing, you may now be able to recognize factors that have contributed to poor sleep during the week that has just gone by. There may have been extra stress at work, project deadlines or arguments at home, or perhaps you've been deliberately staying too busy to think about anything, worrying right up until the time that you go to bed, so then thoughts you've been pushing away come out during sleep when your guard is down.

As you reflect on your sleep notes, you may also recognize reminders that occurred out of the blue and triggered bad dreams later, such as a flash of something that you saw out of the corner of your eye, a remembered smell or sound or being involved in an embarrassing incident. Identifying such triggers can be a valuable step in understanding why your sleep was so poor at a particular time. You have more *clues* to help you put the pieces together, and you won't feel so helpless.

As your sleep attitude begins to shift slightly to the positive, try out new 'coping statements' that could help you feel a bit more in control. These might sound like: *'This is temporary'* . . . *'I am trying out new ways to cope'* . . . *'There are steps I can take to help myself to improve my sleep'*. Try to generate some in your own words and record them in your notebook.

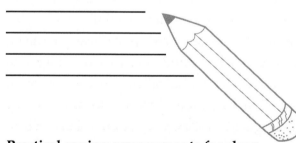

Practical coping arrangements for sleep

◆   Remember to use your managed-breathing skill! The 4–5–6–push breathing method is available for your use at any time, and can be especially helpful as you try to settle down to sleep. Slowly counting as you breathe in through your nose, hold, and breathe out completely through your mouth helps you to settle and turn off some of your 'worry thoughts' about how you'll sleep tonight. If you do wake in a startled, hyper-aroused state, use the 4–5–6–push method to help you re-orientate to a waking state and bring your breathing down to a more normal rate. Remember to blow out forcefully first to begin the breathing rhythm.

◆   If you have a bed partner who has been very disturbed by your PTS reactions during sleep, you may need to make a temporary arrangement to sleep elsewhere in your home, or to move to a different bed or the sofa if you're having a bad time on a particular night. It's useful to explain why you're doing this beforehand (for example, say that you're trying to master new ways of coping with your disturbed sleep and you want to minimize disruption to your partner), so that the other person doesn't feel shut out or rejected when you switch to another spot.

◆   Avoid caffeinated drinks before bedtime, or even from late afternoon onwards, and try as much as possible to establish a routine that helps you relax a bit: this might include listening to soft music, doing mindless tasks like playing computer solitaire, reading a magazine or watching an old, unexciting film or a TV repeat. Use the breathing exercises and even combine them with recorded instructions for relaxation or meditation. It's a good idea to have a little bowl of water and a small towel beside the bed in case you awake sweating and terrified – use the dampened cloth to soothe your face and eyes and help re-orientate you to the waking state. Keep a notepad and pencil beside your bed so that as soon as you wake, you can scribble down a few disturbing aspects of your dreams (and even less disturbing ones) to analyse later.

◆   Although physical exercise is obviously a

good thing, don't do a workout just before bedtime – you'll be too wound up to drop into a deep sleep. If you must nap during the day, jot down in your notebook how often that happens, and notice if it seems to help or interfere with your sleep at night.

Congratulate yourself for every small gain you make.

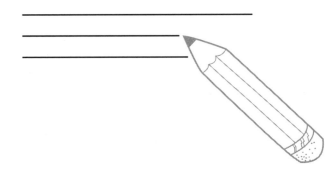

5 Managing Your Anger

The emotional impact of post-traumatic stress will continue to ripple through your life in very intense ways. Like the tip of an iceberg, anger, the most noticeable emotion, will usually be found at the top. Just as powerful, but often hidden underneath, are layers of guilt, grief and loss, and sometimes depression and despair. Recognizing these feelings, acknowledging the thoughts that are fuelling them, and working with CBT exercises to help to change your perspective can be your next challenge.

Just as you've identified triggers that set off your flashbacks and intrusive thoughts, the emotion of anger can be triggered in a split-second, by something very minor that provoked it. In an instant, you're in full 'fight or flight' mode, ready to do battle for your survival (even if the trigger was that someone jammed the photocopy machine or forgot to replace the top on the toothpaste!). Why are you so prone to this type of over-reaction after traumatic experiences? The answer has three parts:

◆ the physical arousal systems in your body;

◆ your interpretation of any challenging,

stressful or aggressive behaviours from others;

◆ the underlying feeling that your assumptions about life, the world and your safety in it have been violated and that nothing is completely safe or can be totally trusted again.

Hyper-arousal is one of the hallmark symptoms of post-traumatic stress reactions (see the list on page 9). Highly emotional events of all types leave traces in the memory, and the catastrophic nature of your traumatic event caused biochemical changes that 'burnt' images and feelings into your memory. Some call this becoming 'hard-wired' in your arousal reactions – it takes only the slightest prodding to set off volatile behaviour. This happens because your autonomic nervous system has become stuck on 'red alert' and even on a subconscious level you continue to scan for danger. Your assumptions about your personal safety in the world, along with your sense of natural justice, have been violated, and it will take concentrated effort, and time, to begin to rebuild a new protective coating on that invisible 'shield' of personal safety that helps us all to function in our everyday lives.

How can I cope when my anger reactions seem to come out in an instant?

Bring out your notebook and, for the next seven days, begin to track every episode of anger or outbursts of irritability that you have, for example:

◆ *When?* Tuesday

◆ *What happened?* Sarcastic comment from co-worker

◆ *What I thought:* He's out to get me . . . he knows how jumpy I am and he's trying to embarrass me.

◆ *How I reacted:* I yelled out in the office, 'I've had enough of your sneaky comments!'

◆ *What I could have done differently:* I should have paused, taken a deep breath, and replied, 'No comment.'

_____

_____

_____

What do you notice?

The advantage of using your notebook to keep track of your angry, irritated and frustrated feelings (even when you're keeping them to yourself and not having outbursts) is that it provides some release and even functions as a silent witness to your struggle to cope with these intense feelings. It also allows you to 'replay' the anger incident in slow motion in your mind's eye, and reflect on how you might respond differently next time you're aggravated. If possible try not to dwell on blame or wishes for revenge, as those thoughts keep you stuck in whatever took place, wanting the other person to realize the error of his/her ways and 'play fair'.

'Justice' rarely comes in the way that you're

hoping for, and you need to move forward in your thinking and realize that, in everyday, annoying interpersonal exchanges, you do always have options to interpret the situation differently and behave more appropriately – not so much for the benefit of the other person but because it keeps things safer for you and allows you to practise getting a better grip on your temper.

'Taking your temperature'

As you continue to work on anger management, it's helpful to look back through your notes and see if you could give each incident when you were angry, frustrated or irritated a number rating from 10 to 100. In this way you're 'taking your temperature' and beginning to pay attention to the difference in your physical and verbal reactions according to how 'hot' you rated the situation.

_____

_____

'Take your temperature' activity

Try to recall and visualize your physical reactions: did your body tense up? Where were you the most tense . . . upper body . . . arms and shoulders . . . neck and face? Did your stomach go into a knot? Were you clenching your teeth? Were you sweating or getting cold? How does your body change when the situation escalates? What about tone of voice? Do you get louder as you get angrier? Now try to picture bringing your 'temperature' down by 10 degrees at a time, starting with the 'hottest' recorded incidents . . . what do you have to do?

It's a good idea to use the 4–5–6–push breathing method, and you may have to talk to yourself in positive, encouraging terms if you know you have to encounter an annoying co-worker or neighbour, etc. If you always over-react to certain things, such as your teenager's messy behaviour, decide that you're going to let that go . . . just for today!

Steps in an anger management strategy for tricky interpersonal encounters could be:

◆ delay (don't say anything right away)

◆ count (backwards, from five down to one – it serves as a distraction)

◆ exhale

◆ breathe

◆ talk slowly

◆ ask questions (get more information, rather than making accusations).

These allow you a few moments to cool off.

Physical exercise is always a good and healthy way to 'burn off steam'. If you wish, you could explore some less-traditional exercise alternatives, such as yoga, t'ai chi, qigong and even salsa dance lessons to teach you to notice how your body moves and reacts under new, positive stimulation, and to help you manage adrenaline rushes.

Caution: If you find you're taking your anger out on yourself, pulling your hair, banging your head, pounding the wall with your fist, driving dangerously or cutting yourself, it's a clear sign that your feelings are out of control and too intense to manage on your own. *Please seek the help of a professional* and remove yourself from people and situations that have the potential to trigger your urges to self-harm.

6 Coping with Guilt

One of the most pervasive emotions in the cluster of post-traumatic reactions is *guilt*. Guilt might arise from having survived in a situation when others have died (known as survivor guilt), or from having escaped or departed from a terrible geographical location when others had to stay behind (for example, journalists reporting from war-torn or disaster-ravaged countries often feel survivor guilt when they return home to peaceful surroundings to file their stories). The thought processes behind guilt often arise from an exaggerated sense of responsibility, where you might think that somehow you had the 'magical' ability to have prevented the terrible thing that happened, and you failed to do so. Your thoughts are peppered with 'shoulds':

❛ I should have known!' . . . 'I should have seen it coming!' . . . 'I should have stopped it in time! ❜

This line of thinking could be termed the 'reverse crystal ball' phenomenon. It intensifies your tendencies to blame and criticize yourself by implying that you were careless and failed to prevent tragedy by not doing enough, even though in reality it would have been impossible to know what was going to happen.

Are there any other thought processes behind survivor guilt – those who don't think they could have prevented something but feel guilty nonetheless, say, for not at least trying to help?

Sometimes traumatized people who have held religious beliefs in God or in a 'Universal Goodness' feel that they have been betrayed by the spiritual forces they believed in, and then feel guilty for having these reactions. Some may feel they have been singled out for bad things to happen to them, and wrestle with guilt because they think they have brought bad luck to others. If you've been experiencing feelings of this nature, talking with a health professional or pastoral counsellor can be helpful.

Coping with guilt: Activity 1

Have a serious 'talk' with yourself on paper, in your notebook, about your trauma-related guilt. Use several columns to fill in your responses to the questions below, and you might even want to ask them out loud, to yourself. Answer as honestly and as bluntly as you can – this is *for your eyes only*!

◆ What was my intention in being there?

Examples: *To enjoy the game; visit my relations; cross the street to help someone; protect my country.*

◆ Did you have mixed emotions about it beforehand?

Examples: *I only went to please my mother . . . I was still hung over and didn't want to drive . . .*

I couldn't concentrate on the road.

◆ What outcome did you honestly expect?

Examples: *We would satisfy the family expectation . . . get through it . . . make everyone happy and come home!*

◆ How much power are you attributing to yourself in the situation?

Example: *If I had been closer, I could have saved him/her.*

◆ Are you guilty for surviving and wanting your life to go on? (*Yes or No*) Explain.

Coping with guilt: Activity 2

The purpose of this activity is to help you examine your guilty thoughts and potentially re-interpret them in a balanced way. Again, use your notebook to make some columns for your answers. Stop if you become overly distressed. You can do a bit more later.

Column 1: Describe your expectations before the event, for example, 'What I thought was going to happen'.

'I expected that we would be at the game laughing, cheering, having snacks, feeling exhilarated and going home together.'

Pause after describing just the content of your expectations.

Column 2: Write, in shortened form, what did actually happen.

'She was pushed by the crowd, fell and hit her head.'

Pause again after describing just the facts, as they occurred.

As you can see, this activity is attempting to help you separate your emotional reactions from the factual content of what actually happened, to assist you in becoming more objective, rather than overwhelmed by guilt.

Column 3: Is there something, however small, about which you can accept that you did the best you could? Don't deny any positive actions or belittle your efforts.

'I called for help.'

Identify any small piece of positive action that you can, and **accept** it.

Column 4: What portion or 'piece' of your guilt can you let go or release yourself from?

'I am only responsible for half of this – the weather was responsible for some of it – the crowd was responsible too.'

Column 5: Can you now **re-interpret** or rename some of the emotions that may go beyond guilt into sadness or other feelings? Try to identify these.

'I feel remorseful . . . uncomfortable . . . sad . . . regretful.'

Can you put your feelings of guilt to the side now, so that they are not 'in your face' all the time? Re-read these notebook entries to help you find a better balance. Make a statement about the present, such as *'I approve of how I am acting in this moment.'* Try to feel good in the here and now. Guilt is *not* a badge of dishonour. You're not 'marked'.

If you feel an urge to make amends, make it a constructive action – do volunteer work, express appreciation to others, channel your energy in newly positive ways, do 'random acts of kindness'. You could re-frame your thinking:

'My guilt is about what I can't change . . . I will allow myself to live peacefully for this moment . . . I do this to help the world.'

7 Understanding Feelings of Grief and Loss

When someone you knew and cared about has died as part of an incident that traumatized you as well, coping with the overwhelming feelings that arise is complicated indeed. Not only are you trying to grieve for the one who was lost, but you're also faced with your own losses: the loss of hopes and dreams, the interruption of future plans, the disappearance of a sense of trust and safety.

Many of the reactions that we have already discussed will be occurring at random for you: sleeplessness, surges of anger, guilt for having survived when a loved one didn't, and these may be accompanied by disbelief, a sense of helplessness and sometimes utter despair. The post-traumatic reaction of emotional numbness may keep you going through the motions, like a robot at times, but all those suppressed feelings do not go away, they stay with you and intrude in your thoughts and behaviour.

Some grief experts suggest that you need to work on and at least partially resolve your own traumatic experience before you can effectively grieve the loss of another. Unfortunately, society expects us to do the opposite – bury the dead, reconcile the loss, be grateful that you survived and, within about six weeks, move on with your life! This type of social pressure from well-meaning individuals is unrealistic and often increases feelings of isolation while you're still grieving.

When you feel able, use your notebook to make two lists: 'Things I miss' and 'Things I don't miss'. These lists might be about a departed one, or about aspects of your life before that are gone now. The purpose is to help you become a little bit objective, and face your feel-

ings a bit at a time. The hardest part for many, and the stage where we often get stuck in grieving, is feeling that we are being disloyal to a loved one if we relax for a few moments, and enjoy something pleasant, without thinking of the one we have lost. We're afraid to forget or to seem as if we have moved beyond our grief and thus portray that our loss was not so important. Sometimes feelings about what has been lost are mixed or ambivalent – there may be relief that the person didn't live to suffer, even though they are truly missed. Try to pinpoint, in your notebook, what is getting in the way of your healing and of resolving your loss.

Even if you've participated in public memorials, it can help to design your own personal goodbye ritual, or private memorial. For example, you may want to write a letter to a departed loved one (even if that was an unborn child or a stillbirth or even one of your own limbs that was amputated), saying how much you cared, how much you miss them, describing how deep are your feelings of loss. Often, there are tears and pent-up emotions released with this activity. You can 'send' the letter by storing it in a private place, burying it or burning it and scattering the ashes.

When the loss involves permanent or semi-permanent changes in physical abilities, facial disfigurement or sensory impairment, most find it difficult to carry on and accept what has happened. Feeling that your body has betrayed you or that fate has betrayed you and questioning whether you want to live with your changed appearance or weakened abilities are normal first reactions. Rehabilitation of your emotional well-being is as vitally important as meeting the physical challenges of recovery. Do not suffer on your own – seek psychological support and accept help if it's available. Your task is to reclaim your body as it is now, and regain a sense of control and purpose.

Anniversary reactions are surprisingly common and may take you by surprise if you feel you've been quite resolved about your traumatic experience. Even years later, things may be going along well, and then, suddenly, you're irritable, sleeping poorly, agitated and upset without knowing why. Ask yourself if you're coming close to an anniversary of the trauma and, if so, your symptoms may make sense and you can expect them to diminish once the actual anniversary date has passed.

8 Overcoming Emotional Numbness and Avoidance Behaviours

Being unable to express loving feelings and respond to others in the way you normally did before your trauma can leave you feeling like a stranger in your own skin. Nothing feels and looks like it did before – you're 'set apart' and may even have brief anxious episodes when you feel like you're outside your own body, watching everyone but separated from them, like being behind a glass wall. With the numbing of your emotional responses, you tend to be caught up in your own world, not because you're intentionally shutting others out but rather, you're preoccupied with the aftermath of your trauma and your usual ways of interacting have been shattered.

Family members may be patient with you for a fairly long time but, after a while, as they watch you staring into space, or looking blank when asked a question about everyday matters, irritation may set in, and they might accuse you of 'not being with it' or being 'totally self-absorbed'. These comments from loved ones may seem to imply that 'a stronger person

could cope better with this', and can cause deep blows to your sense of confidence, resulting in lower self-worth. Your thoughts may be full of self-recriminations and self doubts:

> I'm going crazy and that's why I can't cope . . . I can't count on myself to react appropriately any more!

Your thick wall of emotional scar tissue may keep you feeling like an imposter; for example, you go through the motions, but you continue to believe that, if your loved ones really knew what was going on inside you, they could never accept the 'real' you as you are now. Remember, all of this is commonly felt as part of post-traumatic stress reactions, and therefore, feelings are *not* truth! Keep reminding yourself of that.

While there's a ripple effect of PTS reactions that sometimes causes relationships to break down, as loved ones and friends lose patience with you, you can avoid worsening the situation by reflecting on your current thoughts and behaviour and recognizing whether you're not allowing yourself to be loved again. Just as you have done in earlier CBT exercises, you can identify triggers that are spurring you to avoid closeness/intimacy, perhaps for fear that you'll 'contaminate' your partner if you reveal the horror of your traumatic memories. You may be wary of joining closely with another in case the few protective defences you have left will break down.

Any plan to expose yourself gradually to places, things or people that you've been avoiding since the trauma should be approached cautiously and gently and, if possible, with the guidance and support of a trained professional.

9 Looking Ahead

What can I expect from the future? Will I ever be rid of this?

This booklet has provided you with an introduction to the issues and symptoms that arise with post-traumatic stress reactions. The exercises and strategies to help you overcome your PTS responses are based on cognitive behavioural therapy, a widely recommended treatment style. Some people, especially those who have had a *single* traumatic event, may benefit greatly from the type of self-help approach outlined here, and may even find it sufficient to help them resolve their difficulties. Others, especially those who have experienced ongoing and very complex traumatic situations, such as prolonged abuse, combat exposure or hostage-takings, may find a beginning step here, and the material may help to sustain them while they are working with family doctors or health centres and awaiting referrals to more specific trauma therapy services.

Even when PTS reactions seem quite resolved, they can be re-triggered by large-scale catastrophes, such as natural disasters, acts of terrorism and some of the 'weather terror' that has recently given rise to massive floods and horrible snowstorms, etc. These occurrences seem to betray the natural order of the global climate and may leave you feeling unsafe again. Group support after such events can be helpful in keeping you connected with others and not isolated. As always, it's a good idea to start with your family doctor, to discuss what options are available and what further treatments and other resources may be right for you.

Other Things That Might Help

If you have experienced some benefit from this book but would like to take it further, or if you feel that you need a different kind of approach, don't worry – self-help is not for everyone, and there are many other resources available.

Make an appointment to see your family doctor and ask about alternatives. You may benefit from medication, or more formal therapy. You may also benefit from some help with applying the strategies from a qualified psychologist or health worker, since self-help does work better if you have someone supporting you.

We also recommend the following self-help books:

Overcoming Traumatic Stress by Claudia Herbert and Ann Wetmore, published by Constable & Robinson.

Overcoming Anxiety by Helen Kennerley, published by Constable & Robinson.

Overcoming Depression by Paul Gilbert, published by Constable & Robinson.

Feeling Good: the New Mood Therapy by David D. Burns, published by Penguin.

I Can't Get Over It: A Handbook for Trauma Survivors by Aphrodite Matsakis, published by New Harbinger.

Trust After Trauma: A Guide to Relationships for Survivors and Those Who Love Them by Aphrodite Matsakis, published by New Harbinger.

Life After Trauma: A Workbook for Healing by Dena Rosenbloom and Mary Beth Williams, with Barbara E. Watkins, published by Guilford Press.

The following organizations offer help and advice and you may find them a useful source of information.

UK

British Association for Behavioural and Cognitive Psychotherapies (BABCP)
Tel: 0161 705 4304
Email: babcp@babcp.com
Website: www.babcp.com

Provides contact details for therapists in your area, both NHS and private.

Anxiety Care UK
Tel: 020 8478 3400 (helpline)
Email: enquiries@anxietycare.org.uk
Website: www.anxietycare.org.uk

Mind
Tel: 0845 766 0163
Email: contact@mind.org.uk
Website: www.mind.org.uk

North America

Canadian Psychological Association
Tel: (613) 237 2144
Email: cpa@cpa.ca
Website: www.cpa.ca

American Psychological Association
Tel: 800 374 2721
Website: www.apa.org

Other titles in this series

An Introduction to Coping with Anxiety
An Introduction to Coping with Depression
An Introduction to Coping with Grief
An Introduction to Coping with Health Anxiety
An Introduction to Coping with Obsessive Compulsive Disorder
An Introduction to Coping with Panic
An Introduction to Coping with Phobias

If you'd like to find out more about this series, visit our website at
www.overcoming.co.uk or send an email to enquiries@overcoming.co.uk

The Overcoming series

The *Overcoming* series has helped thousands of people suffering from post-traumatic stress and other problems and many titles are recommended on the NHS 'Books on Prescription' self-help scheme. Subjects covered by the series include:

Anger and irritability

Anorexia nervosa

Anxiety

Anxiety in children

Bi-polar disorder and mood swings

Body image problems and body dysmorphic disorder (BDD)

Bulimia nervosa and binge-eating

Childhood trauma

Chronic fatigue

Chronic pain

Compulsive gambling

Depersonalization disorder

Depression

Grief

Health anxiety

Insomnia and sleeping problems

Low self-esteem

Obsessive compulsive disorder (OCD)

Panic and agoraphobia

Paranoid and suspicious thoughts

Problem drinking

Relationship problems

Sexual problems

Shyness and social anxiety

Smoking

Stress

Weight problems

Worry and generalized anxiety disorder (GAD)

Order now and save money

Quantity	Title	RRP	Offer Price	Total
	An Introduction to Coping with Anxiety (pack of 10)	£29.99	£10	
	An Introduction to Coping with Depression (pack of 10)	£29.99	£10	
	An Introduction to Coping with Grief (pack of 10)	£29.99	£10	
	An Introduction to Coping with Health Anxiety (pack of 10)	£29.99	£10	
	An Introduction to Coping with Obsessive Compulsive Disorder (pack of 10)	£29.99	£10	
	An Introduction to Coping with Panic (pack of 10)	£29.99	£10	
	An Introduction to Coping with Phobias (pack of 10)	£29.99	£10	
	An Introduction to Coping Post-Traumatic Stress (pack of 10)	£29.99	£10	
	An Introduction to Coping with Stress (pack of 10)	£29.99	£10	
	Overcoming Anger and Irritability	£9.99	£7.99	
	Overcoming Anorexia Nervosa	£9.99	£7.99	
	Overcoming Anxiety	£9.99	£7.99	
	Overcoming Anxiety Self-Help Course (3 parts)	£21	£18	
	Overcoming Bulimia Nervosa and Binge-Eating	£9.99	£7.99	
	Overcoming Bulimia and Binge-Eating Self-Help Course (3 parts)	£21	£18	
	Overcoming Childhood Trauma	£9.99	£7.99	
	Overcoming Chronic Fatigue	£9.99	£7.99	
	Overcoming Chronic Pain	£9.99	£7.99	
	Overcoming Compulsive Gambling	£9.99	£7.99	
	Overcoming Depression	£9.99	£7.99	
	Overcoming Insomnia and Sleeping Problems	£9.99	£7.99	
	Overcoming Low Self-Esteem	£9.99	£7.99	
	Overcoming Low Self-Esteem Self-Help Course (3 parts)	£21	£18	
	Overcoming Mood Swings	£9.99	£7.99	
	Overcoming Obsessive Compulsive Disorder	£9.99	£7.99	
	Overcoming Panic	£9.99	£7.99	
	Overcoming Panic and Agoraphobia Self-Help Course (3 parts)	£21	£18	
	Overcoming Paranoid and Suspicious Thoughts	£9.99	£7.99	
	Overcoming Problem Drinking	£9.99	£7.99	
	Overcoming Relationship Problems	£9.99	£7.99	
	Overcoming Sexual Problems	£9.99	£7.99	
	Overcoming Social Anxiety and Shyness	£9.99	£7.99	
	Overcoming Social Anxiety and Shyness Self-Help Course (3 parts)	£21	£18	
	Overcoming Traumatic Stress	£9.99	£7.99	
	Overcoming Weight Problems	£9.99	£7.99	
	Overcoming Your Child's Fears and Worries	£9.99	£7.99	
	Overcoming Your Smoking Habit	£9.99	£7.99	
	P & P		FREE	
			Grand TOTAL	

Name: _____

Address: _____

Postcode: _____

Daytime Tel. No.: _____ Email: _____

How to pay:

1 **By telephone:** call the TBS order line on **01206 255 800** and quote **INTRO-PTS**. Phone lines are open between Monday–Friday, 8.30am–5.30pm.

2 **By post:** send a cheque for the full amount payable to TBS Ltd. and send form to:
Freepost RLUL-SJGC-SGKJ, Cash Sales/Direct Mail Dept., The Book Service, Colchester Road, Frating, Colchester CO7 7DW.

Is/are the book(s) intended for personal use ❏ or professional use ❏ ?
Please note this information will not be passed on to third parties.

Constable & Robinson Ltd (directly or via its agents) may mail or phone you about promotions or products. Tick box if you do not want these from us ❏ or our subsidiaries ❏.